STANDING
IN YOUR
STORM

STANDING IN YOUR STORM

"Navigating Through the
Storms of Life"

DR. JACOB A. SACKEY

Standing In Your Storm
© 2020 By Dr. Jacob A. Sackey
Printed in the United States of America

First Edition

ISBN: 978-0-9894386-3-6

Unless otherwise indicated King James Version
is used throughout this book.

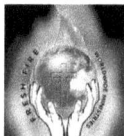

Fresh Fire Worldwide Media
To contact the author, please write to:
Tel. 703-289-9998 / 571-437-4276
Website: www. freshfireworldwideministries.com
Address: P.O. Box 3578
Merrifield Virginia. 22116
USA

Contents

Foreword

Contrary to the widely-held myth in most church circles, being a believer and being anointed does not exclude you from the problems and issues of life. The Lord Jesus Himself tells us we will have trouble in this world. This fact has been proven true year after year. This year has particularly been an eventful one with the arrival of the coronavirus pandemic, which nations and governments in the world over are struggling with how to overcome it.

This book is very timely and a must-have in this season. If you profess to be a believer in a relationship with Jesus as Lord and Savior, you need this book in your life. The author (who happens to be my head pastor and Apostolic Leader-full disclosure) takes an analytical and insightful look at the storms of life. He guides us painstakingly into such segments as the standing of the believer in relation to storms, how storms originate, what storms reveal, and above all what to do when storms arrive. Throughout the work, scriptural backing is provided to buttress the fact that believers are insulated and have divine favor through storms. All we need to do is stand, for the Lord is with us!

This is a highly-recommended reading for every believer. We must always strive to be equipped since we do not know when storms will arrive, and they inevitably will. This book is definitely a giant leap in that direction. I know for a fact that this book will greatly bless your life as it has mine since it began in the form of a sermon series at our local assembly. I for one I am so grateful that Dr. Jacob Sackey made the decision to publish these great truths in book form. May this book always bring you the needed assurance and encouragement and lift your faith up to greater heights in God.

Elder Emmanuel A. Poku
Fresh Fire Worldwide Ministries
Falls Church, Virginia
United States of America

Book Review For Dr. Jacob Sackey

It's amazing what people will try, they will go to astrologers, star gazers, witch doctors, palm readers. They will try everything to see if it's going to be a good day or bad day. But you can't predict the storms.

Storms are impartial, they happen to good people and bad people, the rich and the poor, to believers and unbelievers. They happen to everybody.

Jesus said, "In this world you will have tribulations….." (John 16:33)

"Consider it all joy, my brethren, when you encounter various trials." (James 1:2 NASB)

So it's not if, it's when. Dr Jacob Sackey in his book makes us aware that nobody goes through life sailing easy from cradle to the grave. We all go through tough times. Being a Christ follower does not exempt you from storms.

The author in this enlightening book teaches us on what our response should be when they come and how to make it in a storm.

Remember, there is nothing you will face the rest of your life, even death, that you will face alone. Jesus, if He's in your boat then He is in your life. If you're a believer He is in your boat.

God promises to be with us always even to the end of the age. "I will never leave you nor forsake you."

"But now, this is what the Lord says, He who is your Creator, Jacob, and He who formed you, Israel: "Do not fear, for I have redeemed you; I have called you by name; you are mine! When you pass through the waters, I will be with you; and through the rivers, they will not overflow you. When you walk through the fire, you will not be scorched, nor will the flame burn you. (Isa 43:1-2 NASB)

Gracious Selassie Awoye
Lead Pastor
Treasure House ICGC
London, UK

Endorsement by Dr. F. K. SACKEY, Emergency Physician, UK

A storm is a formidable event to overcome for many a mariner and sea traveller. Being able to weather a good storm is often the test of ones mettle as a mariner or sea farer and though one may be very experienced, the outcome could go either way due to the sheer ferocity of the storm and the power of the sea to subdue all that sail on it. In crunch situations where one has expended all ones expertise and experience, relying on divine intervention is the only option for most.

The apostle Paul was shipwrecked once (Acts 27:27-28:5)and Christ himself was called upon to calm a storm when his apostles cried out in dread (Mark 4:38)

Life's storms are no different! Experience and expertise alone won't get you far in this life without divine help and intervention in some situations. Knowing how to tap into this help or summon this intervention is the key to weathering life's storms as a mariner of the Lord.

Many a myth abounds about what transpires on high seas in great storms and to behold one is to see oneself drawn closer a grim and terrifying end. Picture the master when you are in one of life's similar storms and reach out to Him and He will not disappoint you.

This book will equip you with the tools needed to weather your own storm. Whilst most cower and crouch in fear, you will stand up boldly in the storm knowing that you have the greatest mariner of all behind you as well as the master of the waves on your side. Immerse yourself in it and study it to guide you through your own personal storm.

F K Sackey
MB ChB, Mrcem

Preface

Storms are inevitable. They do not discriminate against anyone. It is not race bias neither does it require a certain level of maturity to be immuned to them. All storms have a duration. They never last a lifetime. If they do, they are not called storms. They are transgenerational demonic harassment. One devoid of such understanding will entertain their state as mainly and solely Gods visitation; Though this may sometimes be the reason one finds themselves in difficult and unyielding situation, the Lord always provides a way of escape for his creation.

Our world is besieged with natural storms which change the landmarks of many countries and create a sense of despair and hopelessness. Spiritual storms are far more devastating in nature because they carry out generational landmarks along with it. The consequences reeled from such destruction if not dealt with from the root can lead to years of instability. Yet our heavenly Father has given us tools to fight and deal with storms whether natural, spiritual or otherwise through the knowledge of the scriptures.

In this book I attempt to deal with at least three most important reasons storms present themselves in our lives and how to successfully navigate through them. Men of honor and integrity according to biblical records like Job (Job 1: 1-2) who lived exemplary lives had been challenged with storms yet in the end The Almighty God sailed him through finding him a better ending. Some storms may produce character checks, it may expose your inert weakness in dealing with any form of pressure. This is important because it reveals one's level of maturity and understanding in life. A person who lacks great understanding, unwilling to be taught and set in their ways will not stay longer in any storm. Navigating away from a storm is the best module for the prudent. Most planes are equipped to handle turbulence however it is not every storm a pilot travel through them. Sometimes they navigate away from very heavy pocket of bad weather for the safety of all. This may prolong the journey, but safety is guaranteed when such steps are taking.

Different age groupings have their own natural storm set in place. A baby teething as compared to an aged person losing their teeth all have storms however, they are handled differently based on the knowledge available.

Let's find out how to deal with the various storms of life and how by the grace of God handle the different stages of our lives.

Introduction

Standing In Your Storm

The Bible teaches in Proverbs 24:10 that "if you faint in the day of adversity, then your strength is small". Thus, if you fail and faint in the day of adversity your strength is very small. It is important to note in dire times like these that we are only kept by the supreme power of God. We are held by God's mercy and grace.

As we examine Matthew's gospel, the eighth chapter and draw some lessons from it, I believe will be insightful and will bless us all in Jesus' precious name. In Matthew Chapter 8 we see right at the onset, Jesus heals a man with leprosy. We find that in verses 1 through 3. Then we see the faith of the centurion from verse 5 onwards. There's a reason why we need to exegete this passage thoroughly so that we appreciate the lessons the Lord will teach in times like these. The Bible then says He heals many, from verse 13 onwards. The Bible further teaches in verse 14 when Jesus came into Peter's house, He saw Peter's mother-in-law lying in a bed with a fever, and He touched her. So far in this chapter, we have seen nothing but good; the healing of a man with lep-rosy, the faith of the centurion being complimented, and the healing power of the Lord Jesus clearly being seen also in the healing of Peter's mother-in-law. Then He begins to talk about the cost for following him.

Right after that, we come to verse number 23. This is to build the basis for the teaching and to let you know that sometimes right after an apparent victory, there comes a situation that makes us even question the presence of God. In victories certain casualties may occur. That should not deter us in celebrating the blessing of God's goodness in our lives. We just celebrated the healing of a leper and of Peter's mother-in-law and the fact that the centurion's faith has just been rewarded. We learn it is going to cost you something to want to follow the Lord. Then in this verse of scripture, which is Matthew 8, and from verse number 23, Bible says:

> *Then He got into a boat, and his disciples followed him. And suddenly a furious storm rose up on the lake so that the waves swept over the boat, but Jesus was sleeping. The disciples went and woke him saying, "Lord, save us! We are going to drown!" And he replied," You of little faith. Why are you so afraid?" Then he got up and rebuked the winds and the waves, and it was completely*

*calm. The men were amazed and asked, "What
kind of a man is this, that even the winds and the
waves obey Him?"*

I want to begin by saying that, a storm reveals essentially
three things in a person's life, particularly during this time
as we're dealing with a global pandemic. Besides a pandemic,
we're dealing with people who have lost their jobs ,political
unrest in many nations , racial bigotry and unrest, the emer-
gence of nationalist groups around the world who do not
embrace the common values of human good whilst others
going through very critical and very difficult situations quite
unsavory and disturbing. This storm too shall pass.

4 | Standing In Your Storm

Chapter One

GOD'S WILL
AND STORMS

First, a storm reveals the fact that you may be in the very center of the will of God.

Contrary to what is typically taught, a storm can and will reveal that a person is in the center of the will of God. The Lord Jesus was in God's will, but the Bible teaches that they nailed Him to a cross. It was the will of God for Him to be killed. It was the will of God for Him to be beaten. Through His beatings, we have our healing as Isaiah 53 clearly points out. We see John the Baptist lose his head through the preaching of righteousness. John was a preacher of righteousness and holiness. He was undoubtedly in the center of the will of God, and yet we saw that a storm rose in John's life. Because of wickedness it only took a dance from Herod's wife's daughter to kill John the Baptist. These are all considered storms when righteousness is rewarded with pain. We equally see John the Revelator, being in the

5

center of the will of God. We are told that he was put into hot boiling oil and thrown to the island of Patmos, left for dead. However, it was on that island that the Lord began to use him and to point him towards revelatory things about the Seven Churches, and how we now benefit from such glorious, insightful revelations that came to him by the Lord and by angels through the Ministry of the Holy Spirit in the life of John. Remember the man Job? He was in the center of the will of God (Job 1). The Bible says he was a righteous and a faithful man. He was a man who served God, but yet he was plagued with many things.

There are times we question whether or not God is with us because we may be going through very dark and difficult circumstances and unfortunately, certain teachings have prevailed that make us begin to question why there is human suffering. Human suffering is as a result of the fact that we live in a depraved world. However suffering does not have to be continuous. Suffering always has a duration. God has earmarked that after we have suffered a little while, the God of all grace through Christ will also strengthen you. (1 Peter 5:10) Remember, the Lord Jesus was the Suffering Servant before He became the Crowned King.

Chapter Two

OPERATING OUTSIDE
THE WILL OF GOD

Secondly, we see that a storm can reveal that a person is outside the will of God.

We find a man by the name of Jonah. The Bible says that God sent him to go to Nineveh to preach, and he boarded a ship going the opposite direction, making sure that he was not going to fulfill the purpose of God. He wanted to walk away, because he considered that Nineveh was not worth repentance and the goodness and blessedness of Jehovah. Right in the midst of that, we see that Nineveh more than likely had people in need, so God had prepared this man. This man Jonah however does not want to be an obedient prophet, so he tries to get away from the presence of God and from his assignment that he was created for. He was walking outside of that mandate and as a result, a storm arose. The Bible says the other passengers on the ship later found out he was the culprit and threw him off. He finally ended up where he was supposed to go.

Now, the third thing is that a storm is a test of our faith.
A storm comes to test the validity of our claims of whether or not we really and truthfully belong to God. By the time this whole situation is over and the dust settles, with governments now beginning to ease restrictions and society slowly beginning to find ways to get back to normal, I dare say that many people who profess Christ, who don't really know him in truth may be found wanting. My simple prayer for you will be that God never finds you in a place completely outside of the will of God. There are many of us that by the grace of God have been blessed with good churches, good pastors, great teaching and a wholesome house of God, but we've taken it lightly until something bad had happened, like this pandemic. The Lord our God is making sure that through this, He is going to test what is in all of us. Real materials are tested by fire, and when something isn't genuine or completely yielded to God's way, God has a way of aligning or birthing that person to coming to His purpose and His plan. God has His way of bringing us into a place of testing and into a place where He shows what we are made up of. There are four things that the believer in the household of God is made up of (2 Timothy 2:20). There is wood, there is silver, there is gold, and there

is stubble. Here, the Bible tells us that fire proves what we are, so in the midst of a storm, we find out who we really are. Without a storm, we may never really know what our stand is on who we claim to say we are. It is during a storm sometimes that we begin to find out our truest identity of who really we are. There is nothing wrong about the testing of our faith. The Bible speaks precisely about the testing of our faith, that there are many people whose faith had been tested, and they have proven themselves. The testing of our faith is called "precious" (1 Peter 1:7).

The other day, somebody asked why was it that whenever they believed God for great things sometimes it turned out very bad experiences. I asked them to go and read the book of Hebrews. The Bible tells us that by faith, many people saw their children sawn asunder, and yet they held on to their faith. There was torture, but they held on to their faith. They went through all kinds of things that would have caused people to loose faith in God, yet they held on to their faith. The Lord wants us to hold on to Him in our moments when the storms are raging.

Chapter Three

BRACE YOURSELF,
JESUS STILL CALMS STORMS

Now we come back to our story in Matthew Chapter 8, when Jesus calms the storm. Now before this, we had nothing but great healings taking place. Right after the storm, we have a man possessed by a demon that Jesus needed to reach. That means that when you come out of a storm, there is always an assignment that is set before you. A storm will never leave you in the same state you were before it, it could make you better or bitter. Before a storm we may be enjoying a time of comfort, happiness, coziness, bliss, blessing, and a time of rest, but after a storm there is an assignment that God sends us to even in our discomforting state. We saw in the early chapters of Matthew 8 that the assignments how the lord Jesus performed miracles with a sense of ease and adjuration. Those were when people were being healed.

A greater attack would come from the powers that controlled the waters. In my book Overcoming Marine Kingdoms much of this is already dealt with. If you cannot confront what is challenging to you in a difficult place, you cannot be trusted to be sent for the greater works. God can never entrust noble ideals to your care if you fail in the smallest assignments. The Lord will give us grace to be able to stand in the times we are living in. The Lord will give you power to be able to perform. The Lord will give you unction to be able to perform. The Lord will give you the fortitude to be able to stand. The Lord will help you so that by the time you come out of your storm, you would have been well equipped to face the assignments ahead of you. May the God of Glory bless you and empower you for service! May God use you now irrespective of wherever you are, wherever you may be. May God allow you to now use the storms and the difficult situations with lessons learnt to be able to birth and bring other people into their God assigned purposes. That is why we are looking at the subject of standing in your storm. Not falling, not quitting, but standing! Being able to stand, being able to have a sure testimony, being able to come out on the other end, and still being an example and being a blessing, still speaking the name of God, still declaring that God is good, still saying that Jehovah is. In Ephesians 6, verses 10 through 12, the apostle is writing to the church in Ephesus. And it says:

Finally my brethren, be strong in the Lord……

"Be strong" implies you can possibly become weak. You can be weak by what you hear. You can be weak by feeding on the negative trends that come daily through that magical box that is in your living room called television. You can become so weakened by looking at statistics of people dying, all the negative things. They are not telling us about the people who are being healed, but there are people being healed as we pray. Yes, there are people being healed. The statistics was pointing to the fact of a colossal loss of lives ,as they were looking at a huge number of people losing their lives. At present thousands of people have perished by the Covid-19 evil virus of our time, yet countless many people being healed and getting better are never reported, They are not telling us much about the fact that mysteriously it seems that heightened curve is now being flattened by the power of God. Our God reigns, indeed He does. God is on the move doing things on behalf of His people, and we are not going to become silent. We are those going to stand and see the salvation of God in the land of the living. The Lord Almighty wants me to let you know that you don't have to become weak. Be strong in the Lord. There are many people who begin to become weak in the time of their storm. They become weak because of what they hear. They begin to become weak because they are around weak people. They begin to fall into weakness because the things they see make them think there is no hope. But there is hope in God. There is power in God, there is deliverance in God. The Lord God of the universe will set you and I free. This pandemic will be over by the grace of Almighty God. You will be secure, you will be well and you will be kept by the power of God.

Now the thing about a storm is that you are either going through a storm right now as we speak, or you have come out of one, or you are about to enter one. In any one of these three phases you may find yourself, I want you to know that God is with us. The Bible says,

> *Lo, I am with you always, even to the end of the age. (Matthew 28: 20)*

So, The Lord Jesus is with us. Jesus is working with us. Jesus through the power of the Holy Spirit is allowing us to walk through these areas, to know His mighty power, to know that indeed, He will be with us throughout our lives' journey. Ephesians says:

> *Finally, my brethren, be strong in the Lord and in the power of His might. Put on the whole armor…. (Ephesians 6: 11)*

Put on the whole armor. Don't put half of the armor on. Put on the whole armor of God, that you will be able to stand against the wiles of the devil. And then it says, *for we wrestle not…* Friends, there is a wrestling going on. Scripture says we wrestle not against flesh and blood, but against principalities, against powers, against the rulers of the darkness of this world, against spiritual wickedness in high places. I say therefore, take unto you the whole armor, not half the armor, the whole armor. Take the whole armor of God with you. Let the Word of God sit with you. Let the power of God work with you. Let the grace of God work with you. Let the Blood of the Covenant be upon your lips and be a covering upon you. Take the whole armor. Take the Gospel, Hallelujah, which is the power of God (Romans 1: 16). Take all of God's armor with you into battle and stand and you will see the hand of God. You will see the power of God. Sometimes as humans, when we are in a battle, or in a storm, we tend to think that we can solve that storm by reason of something we must do naturally without divine assistance. Clearly, as we look around our world, we have seen that people are running everywhere for a cure. They are running and racing for a cure. Governments are in a state of panic. People in high-vantaged positions who never thought that this virus could get to them are getting it. That tells you that humanity is helpless without God. Our storms without God make us very helpless. But when God is in the center, of our lives, we are not hopeless or helpless. We will come out in the end, and will see the Hand of God. Every battle can be won, but not always by natural means. There are battles that are won spiritually and there are equally battles that are won in the natural through the application of wisdom. There are some things that are way above human understanding. They are way above science. They are way above logic, reasoning and rationale. They are way above where you and I would estimate. For example, a person may attain a very high level of education, and yet will not be able to become a contributing person in society. A person may come from a good home and may end up on the street. A person may start well, and may seem to have been rocked by different turbulences of life, and no one will clearly understand why it is so. This clearly is a work of darkness, and a wrestling in the spiritual dimension.

Chapter Four

OVERCOMING DEMONICALLY
ORCHESTRATED STORMS

Demons thrive on the fact that there are storms. The Bible tells us that in Matthew 8, that a storm arose and when it did, Jesus alone was sleeping in the hinder part of the boat. Now if you have read my book on the Marine Kingdom and the power of this invisible world, you will understand that the powers of the sea are the most wicked of all demons. These are powers that try to strive with man on earth because they are very jealous of God's creation. When the Lord Jesus was awoken from sleep and rebukes the raging sea but spoke to the sea. If you read your Bible carefully, it says He spoke to the sea. Now does the sea have an ear? It means there is something behind a storm that the natural mind sometimes cannot work through with logic and reasoning. The human carnal mind cannot bring about a resolve to many of life's ill. But there is an invisible power of God that will, when the believer taps into that, in the time when storms arise, that the believer can experience, that the believer can come into, that the believer can realize God's potential power and the Hand of God. So here, we understand that not every battle can be won in the natural. God makes you hopeful and gives you adequate resources to be able to stand in the midst of a storm.

In 2 Corinthians 4: 4-6, it says the weapons of our warfare are not carnal. The believer has been given weapons by the Lord. Your weapons are not in your money. Clearly you may have money and not be able to go anywhere at this moment. The weapons of the believer are the potency of the Word of God, the potency of the Blood, the potency of the Name of Jesus. The believer has been given weapons for warfare that are not carnal or humanly devised, but they are mighty through God to pulling down strongholds. God is delivering somebody out of a hopeless situation. You are caught up in a storm, and you think that you are never going to come out of the storm? But I'm here to tell you that God is going to bring you out and is going to make you shine as He gives you a better and a bigger assignment. Just as the Lord Jesus overcame the storm and went and made an evangelist out of a demon-possessed man, so also will the Lord God commission and send you for greater works in His Holy Name. The Lord will equip you and empower you for greater service in His Holy Name. Isaiah 54 and verse number 17 says no weapons formed or forged against you shall stand. So weapons are formed to destabilize us in a storm. But it says no weapon formed against you shall prosper. No weapon, formed, fashioned, directed against you shall prosper; say that out loud!!! The weapon of hopelessness, the weapon of negativity, the weapon of disease, they shall never prevail over the redeemed child of God. I declare to you as a man of God, no weapon formed against you shall prosper by the grace of God. The Lord of heaven and earth will deliver you and break the weaponry of darkness over you. Remember 2 Corinthians 10: 4-6 tells us that our weapons are not in the natural realm. They are not humanly devised; In times of hopelessness, when there is a great storm brewing and rising, we must understand that God is with us and we are not going under. We are going to come up on the top. We are going to see the good of God in the Name of Jesus. We are going to see the Hand of God in the midst of all this. At the end of the day, it is Jesus whose hands have already been raised over our lives. May I tell you that His Hands are not going to be raised? They were raised at Calvary. They were raised, the Bible says, when He destroyed all principalities and powers in his death. He raised Adam's fallen race in his death. He destroyed the power that held us ransom and that is why no weapon formed against you shall prosper. You can stand in your storm. You can stand and see the salvation of God in your storm.

Nahum 1: 7 says:

> *The Lord is good. He is a stronghold in the day of trouble.*

The Lord is good! God is our storm preserver. He is our stronghold. He is our wall of defense. The Lord is our shield. The lord is our stronghold in the day of trouble. Are you in trouble? Do you find yourself in trouble? Do you find yourself in a place of abject barrenness where nothing is happening, nothing is going on? Then I want you to be hopeful because the Bible says the Lord is good. Every good and perfect gift cometh from the Lord above (James 1:17). Religion wants to make God look bad. Problems that people do not understand are pinned on God to make God look bad. But the Bible says that God is good (Psalm 100:5). And He is a stronghold in the day of trouble. He is our stronghold. Blessed be His Holy Name.

You need to gird your loins and you need to be able to stand in the day where there is a storm. The claim of your love for Jesus, that claim of your validation in God stems from the fact of storms, when storms come. That is where we prove the fact that we love Him. Those who have gone ahead of us lived in times when they were thrown to lions. Some were thrown into fires and some were placed in prison unjustly. We live in times where people live in the corridors of freedom and comfort, in air-conditioned churches and paneled places, in soft tissue chairs. There are those serving God who do not have even a chair to sit on. Yet we complain about everything. May God allow us to understand that serving Him may sometimes bring us into a place where a storm may arise, but if the storm does arise, it proves we would stick and stay in our allegiance to him. We pledge allegiance now to the Blood of the Lamb. We pledge allegiance to Him that in life, in death, in difficulty, in lack, in abundance, in whatever situation we may find ourselves, we will serve the Lord until the end of our time. Let not our Christianity be based upon what we get from God. Let it be based upon what He through us can bless our world by. It is cheap Christianity, to only be after houses and lands and cars and things and never leave a legacy of an imprint of the God in you here on earth. May the Lord let you understand that though the enemy may try to use and utilize a storm for his campaign, He will bring you out shining better, blessed, and blissful for the glory of God. You know the Book of Job starts with a man who lived righteously and is then rudely interrupted with a storm, but may I tell you the end of the Book of Job? The Bible says that God gave to Job twice of everything that he lost (Job 42:10). May God give you double of everything that you have lost in the name of the Lord! When we come out of this pandemic, may God find you standing. May you stand in the midst of your storm, and may you be a true soldier of Jesus Christ, bearing testimony of the fact that you loved Him in the pandemic, and that you love Him outside of it. Whether pandemic or no pandemic, we pledge allegiance to the Lamb, and we bear our loyalty to the Blood of the Lord Jesus Christ, that He who saved us and He who shed his blood for us , He who redeemed us is worth serving even to death. Praise the Lord! A time is coming in many countries not too long from now, that storms would rise as the Bible has in many places predicted. A time is going to come that the Bible is going to be thrown aside, the church mocked as outdated and irrelevant , that is the more reason for us to begin to dig into the Word of God and become a people who are very conversant with the promises and patterns of Gods dealing with things in the universe. As the people of God, it will be well noted that we are a people that know the Word of God, who will not be tossed to and fro by every wind of doctrine that comes about. We will be able to stand in our storms and take a firm standing against all odds.

Chapter **Five**

THE GOD OF ALL
COMFORT

Psalm 107: 28-31 says:

Then they cried unto the Lord in their trouble,
And He brought them out of their distress.

T here was a time in the life of the Children of Israel, in the land of their captivity and bondage, where there were no exits because the only thing that could allow them to pass was a body of water. How were they going to cross? The Egyptians were mightier than they were. The only passage over to the other side where they could go also was with water. How were they going to carry their children and possessions? How were they going to do it? But they did not need to swim. God parted the waters and allowed them to walk on the seabed. That's who our God is, the God who parts waters will do the same for you. Growing up as a young evangelist brought upon me many testing and trials, I once heard a notable person I respected had given up on me. They had written me off like a bad debt, yet the ensuing years would prove otherwise. If only you can stand the test of your time you will see the glory of the Living God. Back in the days I had a three tone shoes suitable for any outfit, those experiences have guided me to help countless many whom others have written off. I remember once grinding hot pepper and salt to eat with a staple diet. No meat or protein at the time, however troubles do not always last. God will make a way of escape for you.

God will let you walk on firm ground amid your storm and you will get to the other side by the power of God. You will not die in the place where the enemy thinks your storm is brewing. You will actually come out better for the Name of God and for the testimony of Jesus Christ.

Again, let's look at Psalm 107: 29:

> *He maketh the storms a calm so the waves thereof are still.*

God makes the storms become calm. God will also make your storm become calm. Does it seem to appear that the work of your hands has shrivilled and come to a halt? God will make that storm calm. I speak to you prophetically now in the name of The Lord, that there's going to be the changing of the guard at the end of the day. It is going to be far more beneficial and better when we come out of this. You are going to see that the Highest God has preserved you and I indeed. May the Lord make you double in all things by the time we come out! May the Lord make you shine above all things. May the Lord cause His dazzling glory to be upon you. May the Lord showcase his glory on you. Before this pandemic is over, God will place oil, glory, power and favor upon you. May it be like as in the days of the children of Israel, when they went to their former captors and required of them to give them silver and gold. By the time you open your mouth, favor would have already located you by the power of God. Your storm is preparing for you your Canaan. God is about parting the waters. He is about making you to go on dry ground. God is about leading you out of your land and place of captivity into a place of fulfillment and land that flows with bliss and with milk and honey; This is your portion to receive in the name of the Lord Jesus, that no good thing, the Bible says, will God hold back from them that walk uprightly with him (Psalm 84:11). May the Lord bless you and quicken you to this understanding that your storm would be over by the help of God. By the time this global pandemic is over and the dust settles, you will be standing up by the grace of God. You would not have been tattered and broken to pieces not found wanting in the things of God. No, it won't be your portion. You would be a person who would not lose any respect, no! that will not be your portion. You are going to be a person who will stand still and see the salvation of the Living God. The Bible says He makes the storms a calm, and God will make your storm a calm. You are going to stand in the midst of this storm and see the Hand of God. Yes, the Hand of God shall appear onto you, and God shall do you good in the name of Jesus, Hallelujah. Psalm 107: 30 says,

> *Then are they glad because they be quiet, For He bringeth them to their desired haven.*

God will bring you to your desired haven, Glory Hallelujah! God will not leave you in the center. God will not lead you into the middle. No, but God will take you through it. Just this afternoon I came to a crushing realization and I'd like to share that with you. If the Lord Jesus had not exercised Himself in carpentry, He could not have become a king. Jesus was a carpenter before He became a king. You have to build something in order to rule over it. You have to have gone through a storm in order to have a testimony. If you have not gone through a test, there will be no testimony. There will be nothing for you to showcase about the living power of God. We go about saying, God is good, God is mighty, God is powerful. Now He has given us an opportunity to prove that He is good? This is a time to stand. Verse 31 says,

Oh, that men would praise the Lord for His goodness,

And for His wonderful works to the children of men.

Oh that we would praise Him, because we are coming out of the storm. Yes, we are going to come out in the name of Jesus! Your storm could be in the form of fear, but Jesus is walking with you right this moment and saying to you, "Lo I am with you always, even to the end of the age". The Lord is healing you now. You may have lost everything. I mean everything. But you are going to get everything seven times back in the name of the Lord. These are not wishful thoughts. These are declarations from the throne room perspective. It is the Word of God and the scriptures cannot be broken. If God did it for Job, God will do it undoubtedly for you and me. May God restore to you your lost fortune in the name of the Lord Jesus Christ.

Chapter Six

STRENGTHENED IN
DIFFICULT TIMES

C an you be able to stand during a storm? Can you be able to serve the Lord in the midst of a storm? In most of our situations, our emotions are in disarray. We do not quite know how to process things. But God is visiting you this day, to encourage your heart and mind that the Lord will ride upon your waves. He will give you power, but it is going to require Faith. Remember when the Lord in Matthew 8: 24-26 rose up and rebuked the sea, and spoke to the winds? Afterwards, He turned to the disciples and said to them "Oh ye of little faith" (verse 26). It means that lack of faith can keep you in the storm longer. Oh yes, lack of faith in the providence protection of God and in the provision of God can keep you in a storm longer. When the storm rolled, though He spoke to demons and the powers of the sea, yet the Lord addressed them and said, "Oh ye of little faith".

Faith is going to become an essential ingredient for the child of God. You are going to need faith, not just will power. Man's will power has what it does. You are going to need faith in God and in the invisible power of God. When somebody is under depression, it is not willpower that breaks them out of depression. It takes faith, faith in God to say, "Lord, just like the disciples, I want to believe, but I can't help my unbelief". When faith comes and enters into the heart of a person because they hear the words of faith, God's mighty power rises in the inward part of you. You are able to say: "Even in the midst of this storm, I'm going to serve the Lord. I'm going to stay, stand and wait for my day, until God brings my change. I'm not going to quit, I'm not going to quit. I'm not going to quit!". Faith is essential. You may prolong the duration of your storm by negativity, but you can shorten it by faith. The disciples prolonged the storms on the sea by their doubt, and for as long as they doubted, even though Jesus was with them, the Bible says that the sea raged and beat upon their boat and shook them in their emotions. When the Lord reached out and addressed the spiritual powers of the sea, He turned to them and said, "Oh ye of little faith!" It means greater faith can calm a storm. When a person has been through greater things and are hearing somebody else's small story, thing sounds so small to you. You are able to give guidance because you have been through it. For faith to be activated, one needs to nurse Hope. People think that hope is a very weak word. No, hope is not a weak word. Hope is an important participle that breeds faith in a person's heart. If I'm hopeful for tomorrow, if I'm hopeful that things are going to work, then I give a foundation to the operation of faith. That faith can work inside me. The Bible tells us in the Book of Hebrews 11: 1:

Now faith is the substance of things hoped for.

When you are not hopeful you will come out in the midst of the storm, when everything seem hopeless, then faith cannot thrive. I want to submit to you that if you will ask God to increase your faith, He will. But you have to be hopeful because hope gives the platform for faith in God to be activated. Faith in God will calm your soul. It anchors the soul. Faith in God releases strength. Faith in God is essential for overcoming every storm. Faith is needed to ride the storm. Faith starts with hope. You cannot be hopeless and be hopeful and faithful. You have to be hopeful that God will do what He says He will do.

I just want to let you know that your storm will bring you out better. This storm will bring you out firmly standing for God's glory. The storm will birth out of you greatness. This pandemic will bring the better part of you. By the time it is all over, the glory of God will be so strong upon you. This is our time of incubation. This is our time of prayer.

It is that time of consecration. It is our time of searching the scriptures, our time of getting closer and closer to God. This is our time of understanding the mind of God. As long as we have keyed into this time of great confusion and misery in our world, we would use the time to build on our spiritual levels, spiritual matter, spiritual fabric, and the anointing of God upon us would have increased. May the Lord build in you a reservoir of his power. May God give you stamina. The Bible says if you cannot run with footmen then forget about running with horses. This time will show that it pays to serve the Lord Jesus Christ. I speak from a strong apostolic vein to you, that goodness and mercy will follow you all the days of your life. This pandemic will not take you and your family out in the Name of the Lord. May the crown of life be upon your head now. May it revoke the sentence of early death in the Name of the Lord Jesus Christ. I pray now in Jesus Name by the power of the Holy Spirit, that the Lord Adonai birth in you resiliency, to stand and see the salvation of God. You are not going under; you are standing to ride the storm. You are not going under, no, you belong to the Lord above. You will ride on top just like the boat He rode on top of the storm. You will also ride the storm and come to your safe haven because God has a great assignment for you on the other side. May the Lord anoint you in these difficult times. The Bible says it was in the times of famine that Isaac went out to sow. In these times that nobody extends their hands to do anything for you, may there be a miraculous moving of God on your behalf in the name of the Lord. May you receive from God miracles that you cannot begin to explain because God is God. Receive the touch of the Lord, receive the Hand of the Lord, receive the glory of the Lord, receive the bounty of the Lord, receive the deliverance of God, receive God's mighty power, receive the work of your hands again, be restored to your full capacity and over in the name of the Lord! May the anointing that oozes out of you be an anointing that nobody can question any longer. May the glory that comes out of you amid your storm be such that no one can question it at the end of it. May the Hand of God be upon you, and may the Hand of God do you good.

Chapter Seven

SHAPED THROUGH
DIFFICULTIES

Just as we learnt from Matthew 8, times like these start off with great things. We started the year by God saying He was going to do a new thing. Yes, surely, He's doing a new thing. In the midst of a pandemic your prayer momentum has increased. Our quest and thirst for God in isolation has been greater than it has ever been. Our desire and willingness to go further and beyond is been far expressed now. We see particularly in Matthew, in the eighth chapter, from the beginning, that good things had happened. Then there was a cost to discipleship. Now remember that anytime that God takes you on a journey, it is not necessarily for you alone. The journey and the lessons of life are not to be contained in us alone. God has an express intent that other people may benefit from the expression of His grace and love through what you may have experienced. Though the experience may have been something ugly, something untoward, it is permitted by God. It is working for our good. Though Satan sometimes may use the opportunity, it is the wish of God to use that same thing to bless human beings, to bring people to the place of redemption and power.

We now turn to the Book of Job. Before we do, let me finish this thought so we can understand and appreciate the value of God's Word in helping us stand in times of great difficulty. The Bible says in Matthew 8 that the disciples were with the Lord, and they were on their way to the other side. For anyone who has walked closely with the Lord, we know that when we walk with Him, He makes impossible things possible. When we walk with God, we see glory, anointing and power. How many of us also understand that sometimes we also meet storms? Yes, when we walk with the Lord. There are people who walked with God in times before us that were thrown to the lions. Some of them were cut in two. Others did not deny the testimony of Christ and were not willing to die the same way the Master died, but rather requested that they be burned upside down because they were not worthy of their Master. Therefore, I need for you to understand that before you come into an arena, a place where God can actually utilize your gifts and talents and abilities, God would have to pass you through something. Without going through a storm, you cannot be carved out. You cannot be that person that God can give to your world.

Remember when Jesus took the bread, He took it from that young lad, He blessed it. That is where many of us are, the 'Bless Me' club. But the Bible says He also broke the bread. We must come to the point where we accept that not only does He bless us, He also breaks us. Yes, He allows us to go through the mill, through storms, to go through times of great difficulty. This does not mean He does not care. It does mean that He is developing in us a certain level of resiliency, so that we can become a blessing not only to our world, but to and through people around us for His glory. We want you to understand today that God's purposes go beyond your difficulties. The Bible says affliction shall not come twice. This means that two individuals must not suffer the same plight twice, so what you are suffering for, is for someone else's betterment. The Lord Jesus died so we died no more. The Lord Jesus was crucified on the cross so we were not. The Lord on high was lifted, so we do not lay lifeless in our tombs. Wherever there is no pain, there will be no gain.

WHAT DO STORMS
REVEAL?

Storms in life reveal essentially three things. Number One, storms in life reveal that you are in the center of the will of God. How can you be in the center of God's will and have storms brewing, have children going wayward, have a home that you don't desire to want to be in? How can you be in the center of the will of God, doing everything that you know so well to do? After we have gone through these three, I will give you the two points that will let you know when you're going through a storm whilst you are in God's will. Secondly, the storms that come to us sometimes come by reason of the fact that we are outside the will of God. Joseph was in the will of God, but he was imprisoned. When one finds themselves in the will of God does not mean they may not go through storms. The Lord Jesus was in the express will of the Father, yet he was crucified on Golgotha. John the great prophet, the Baptist, had his head cut off, by reason of being in the will of God. Jeremiah was in God's will but he was left to die in a pit. Joseph son of Jacob was in the perfect will of God, he suffered at the hands of his jealous brothers, and ungrateful prisoner and challenge from Potiphar's wife. For those of us who think the will of God does not allow us into storms, I want you to think again. Sometimes on the onset of walking actually into the will of God, you are met with all kinds of craziness, but that is where you as a child of God need to understand that God is with us and God will help us. So, when you are in the will of God, you can face a storm.

When one finds themselves outside the will of God, they can face a storm. Thirdly, we talked about the fact that there is a testing of your faith which scripture gives a qualifying word "precious" in relation to our faith. Storms bring about one knowing the fact you are in God's will. Secondly, knowing the fact you may not be in God's will. And thirdly, that is to be a test of your faith.

Now, here it is. In all the three key points mentioned, there are two key important things to remember. If I am obedient to the Word of God and I'm going through a storm, I am in God's will. If I am disobedient to the Word of God, and I am going through a storm, it is not God's will. It is as a result of stepping outside the hedge of protection and when I step outside the hedge of protection I become open to ravenous beasts, darkness and satanic elements. I'm open to all kinds of things. Thirdly, the fact that you are obeying the Word of God does not mean you will not be tested. No one ever graduates from college without being tested. No one is ever given a certificate without being tested. For as long as I've been alive, I've come to know there is only one college that they give you a certificate before you start, and that is marriage. Undoubtedly, we know how painful it can become when you are either prepared for it or are met with a misfortune. It is a school of discovery. It makes philosophers out of men and develops women into perpetual silence. In the thing called marriage which Satan hates it is his purpose to make sure that we walk groping in our homes with long faces. That is why you are given a certificate before you start. For all other tertiary courses of study, you write an exam, you qualify for the degree and it is conferred on you. After you have learned and mastered it, you are given a certificate or citation to say that you went through a storm, the storm of learning and we know that you have it. It is only marriage that you discover as you keep going. It could be thirty years and you would still be discovering. You will live in full discovery until you leave the earth. I am not discouraging you about marriage. I'm just saying though, that through the storms that come like that, God gives us wisdom. We can increase and become adequate in our knowledge and our understanding of the things of God.

Chapter Nine

FIGHTING DIFFERENT BATTLES
WITH GOD'S WISDOM

W e stated that not every battle can be won by natural means. I'm just going about some of the things that have already been taught. 2 Corinthians 10: 4-6 tells us the weapons of our warfare are not carnal, but they are mighty through God. This means that the believer has weapons when you are going through times of great strain, stress and storms. The weapons or our warfare are not carnal, but mighty in God and through God to pulling down strongholds, casting down arguments (thought formation and patterns), and every high thing that exalts itself against the knowledge of God, bringing every thought into submission. About 80% of the storms we never get out of is as a result of the fact that because we have been so much singed by the heat of the storm, we tend to culture our minds to stay in that same place even when God has broken the cage wide open. When you cage an animal for a long time, that animal gets conditioned to stay in that place. Even though you may open the cage it will never come out. There's a thing called the mind. Verse 4 tells us that the weapons of our warfare are not humanly devised or carnal. They are mighty through God to pull down strongholds. Then verse 5 says, "casting down arguments and every high thing that exalts itself against the knowledge of God, bringing every thought into captivity, to the obedience of Christ, and being ready to punish all disobedience" when your obedience, when my obedience is fulfilled. Now I said that there are three groups of people: those coming out of a storm, those going into a storm, or those currently in a storm, but whichever area you think you are in, there is deliverance in Mount Zion. Amen, Praise God! Isaiah 54: 17 says, "No weapon formed against you shall prosper and every tongue which rises against you in judgment, you shall condemn. This is the heritage of the servants of the Lord and their righteousness is of me, says the Lord" Then we went through Psalm 107: 28-31.

"Then they will cry out to the Lord in their trouble and He brings them out of their distresses" He calms the storm. The Lord Almighty does that. He calms the storm so that the waves are still. He calms every storm. God will calm your storm. Oh yes, God will calm your storm. Verse 29 says God calms the storm so that the waves are still. And then verse 30 says, they are glad, because they are quiet. So He guides them to their desired haven. Oh, that men will give thanks to the Lord for His goodness, and for His wonderful works to the children of men. Blessed be the Name of the Lord.

Now, we said also that the duration of your storm can sometimes be as a result of little faith or no faith. In Matthew 8: 24-26 the Lord Jesus addresses their situation. *Suddenly a great tempest arose on the sea, so that the boat covered with the waves, but He was asleep. Then His disciples came to Him and awoke Him saying, "Lord, save us, we are perishing". But He said to them, "Why are you fearful? Oh, you of little faith!" Then He arose and rebuked the winds and the sea, and there was great calm.* You can stay longer in the storm by nursing little faith or no faith. You can cut through a storm by standing on the promise of the Word of God to say "Come hell or high water, I know God will pull me out of this" When you stand on a threshold of faith, no storm can overcome you. Storms will come, but they will not overcome you. If you do not stand on the precipice of faith, to believe the power and the promises of God however, the storms will come, and they will stay longer. The storms came whilst Jesus was with them in the boat, and the Bible says it almost overturned their boat. Now you can have Christ walking with you and still have storms. Storms are not indicative of the absence of God, but rather the fact of the presence of God, that though you may be going through storms, and other people may be ridiculing you and be questioning why you are this and that and the other, I came to encourage you, to let you understand that Jesus could be in your boat and yet there could be a storm brewing. There could be something working against the norm but at the end of the day, you are going to rise above it, and God is going to give you the victory. God is going to give His people the victory after this pandemic in the Name of the Lord Jesus Christ. Can you imagine that the Lord was in the boat, and the winds rose up their ugly heads? Can you also imagine in 2020, the believer who walks with God, speaks in tongues, prays six hours a day, gives their tithe, gives their offering, makes sacrifices, does all the things that any person committed to the things and ideals of God wants to do, will face a storm? I came to encourage you. Do not allow your faith to become little. Your faith only weakens when you do not feed on the totality of the promises of His Word, because the Bible teaches Faith only comes by hearing and hearing by the Word of God (Romans 10:17). When the Lord Jesus went into the city called Nazareth, He would not do many miracles there because He could not find them in faith (Matthew13:58). At least little faith is better than no faith. Little faith allows you to call on the Master, but I want us to graduate from little faith to strong faith like Father Abraham. The Bible says that against all odds, Abraham hoped against hope, and believed God was able (Romans 4:18). I also believe God is able. The Church of God is not going down. The Church of God is going to rise through this tidal wave uncertainly and gloom. The powers of darkness are going to bow down in the Name of the Lord Jesus Christ.

Chapter Ten

THE TRIUMPHANT
CHURCH OF CHRIST

The triumphant Church of Jesus Christ is going to emerge out of this, for victory belongs to Jesus. On a hill far away stood an old rugged cross. Why are we talking about the cross? Because that cross stripped our shame, that cross paralyzed the powers of darkness, the cross made sure there would be an empty grave. The cross gives me faith and relevance for the ascension and for the adjudication of my case before the right hand of the justice of the throne of God. By the cross I cannot stay in crisis, for the cross crosses crisis. On that hill the Lord Jesus paid the price of the world. Whilst He was paying the price of the world, the Bible says the earth and the whole heavens became darkened (Mark 15:37-39). A storm arose. The whole heavens became darkened because the sin weight was placed on Him. The very Son of God, rejected, forsaken on a cruel cross, beaten to a pulp. He who had turned water to wine was offered vinegar. On that cross, momentarily as the storm blew, earthquakes and all, the Father turned His face away from His Son, and out of a dying King echoed these words in eternity: "My Father, why hast Thou forsaken me?" (Matthew 27:46). Could You be that anointed of God? Could You be the Son of God? Could You be the very Son of God and feel rejection from God? What would you call it? Would you call it the fact that You stood for God, you healed the sick, you raised the dead, You unstopped deaf ears, You did many things for Him, and now God rejects You? My friend, there is a story behind the death. The story behind the death is greater than the death itself. The story behind the death is that He the Lord Jesus ever lives (Hebrews 7:25); He died once, but He ever, permanently, eternally lives, and can you too, right now, in this moment, in this kind of situation we find ourselves in. You may go through a season of death, rejection, a dark season of being ostracized, a season that people do not even give relevance to your presence, I dare say that resurrection morning is coming, and your relevance shall be celebrated by all, even enemies who do not like you. They will celebrate the gift of God in you.

There are people who are not praying any more. They are not reading their Bibles any longer. They are not witnessing any more. A season is coming up that will reveal truly who you and I claim we are. When the dust settles, you better be found back with God.

Proverbs 24: 10 says if you faint in the day of adversity your strength is very small. There are people who are scared more of a virus than they are of God. Little faith will not cut it in this season. Feed on the Word of God. You will grow in quantum by faith. Faith in God anchors the soul. Faith is an essential commodity during this period and is needed in every storm. Faith starts with hope. Hope is necessary for faith to work (Hebrews 11: 1). Proverbs 13: 12 says: *Hope deferred makes the heart sick, but a dream* (faith) *fulfilled is the tree of life*. Therefore, do not kill the hope you have. You are going to go over by the power of God. After the Lord Jesus rebuked the sea and calmed the storm in Matthew 8, there was a man in the region of Gadara waiting for Him. If you cannot stand the storm, you cannot get to your Gadara. If you cannot stand the storm and beat the storm with great faith, you cannot get to your Gadara, your greater assignment. Storms birth giants out of people. Storms only kill midgets. A storm will reveal whether you are a giant or a midget.

There are benefits of a storm. But we proceed with this, I want to stress that every storm, whether natural or spiritual, has a duration or a time limit. In the (1918-1920) millions of people died of the Spanish flu but God still allowed people to be born. The corona virus pandemic will stop one day because God has the final say-so and will not suffer the enemy to destroy everything He has made according to (Psalm 24:1).

Chapter Eleven

BENEFITS OF STORMS

Now on to Job. We know the story in Chapter 1 the book of Job of how an upright man was confronted with a major storm in his life. In Job 42: 2 onwards, Job says: *"I know that You can do everything, and that no purpose of Yours can be withheld from You".* I know that through my pain, my disease, my mess, my lack, neglect, lonesomeness and affliction, you can do everything. This is the declaration of a person who has been through a lot of attack and havoc caused by the enemy, a person who has been tested and still remains committed to the ideals of Jehovah! The purposes of God will not be truncated! He is ever present in times of trouble, the Bible says.

What are the benefits of a storm? We should not look only at the negative aspects. Here are a few blessings we realize in difficulty.

1. It draws people to prayer. You pray more when you are in a storm. In captivity, the Bible records Daniel prayed three times a day.

2. A storm reunites families. When someone dies, family members who have not spoken for years end up talking.

3. In storms, revivals are born. Souls begin to want to praise and lift up their God and there is a reawakening. No revival has ever been created on its own. Revivals are started by men and women.

4. In storms, the earth is renewed. As the earth slows down, the atmosphere is clear, the air is cleaner, and the environment is fresher. The Bible says God uses snow and rain to renew the earth. It is about to rain the blessing of The Almighty. Your storm and captivity will soon be over. Your season of decay, confusion and drought shall be over. The power of God will put you on a pedestal of glory.

5. A storm is an equalizer. It does not differentiate between poor and rich, male or female, black or white. Just like the grave, a storm allows all of humanity to understand that we are nothing but dust and clay.

A poor man's storm may not be the same as a rich man's storm, but both are in storms.

So what is your storm? What are you facing? Could it be a man? A woman? Is it your finances? Your health? Your child? A relative? A mean neighborhood? Whatever it is, storms do not last. People of faith do. You are going to outlive your storm and you are going to bring glory to God and honor to His Name.

Chapter Twelve

GODS POWER
IN STORMS

So far we have established the fact that storms come essentially, for three reasons. Number One, they come because we are in the center of the will of God. Number Two, they may come by reason of being outside the will of God. Number Three, they come to test our faith. They come to test our faith in the God we proclaim to love.

Though storms will not be desired, not every storm is bad. The storms in Joseph's life landed him finally in the palace. Your storms, though they may seem to be something that would cut you off, will bring you to the set place that God has assigned and designed for you. So we have established that storms do come and they are inevitable. They are part of growth, a part of developing and maturing. In fact, for anybody who wants to forge ahead, you must expect a storm. For anyone who wants to embrace tomorrow, they must understand that there are storms that come with the tomorrow. It is not so much about the storms; it is about who is with you in the storm. That makes a whole difference.

We have talked about the benefits of storms. You would not think that storms have some benefit. First, **storms draw people to prayer**. The second benefit is that **they reunite families**. Basically, a storm brings about re-orientation. It allows people to find their proper bearing in life. It makes them major in the major and minor in the minor. It helps define people. It makes fine people out of very bad and very scary situations. Thirdly, **revivals are borne**; revivals are unearthed by reason of storms because men learn to bow their knee to the Almighty. We said that prayer is like vapor that rises up from the earth and builds to form clouds in the Heavens. We said that the more vapor there is in a particular area, the more it is for us to expect greater rain. The Amazon Forest is known to have rain all the time because it is a dense thick forest. Fourthly, we say **the earth is renewed through storms**. You realize that when a tornado or hurricane or something similar comes in, lives may be lost, which is not an easy thing. Yet people's resolve makes them ever so committed to building new buildings, sometimes even skyscrapers. Storms build fortitude and resiliency on the earth and the men that dwell in it because God would have renewed it and given them a certain zest for life and living. Also, **storms allow us to know our limitations, to know that we are mortals**. No matter what gifts operate in your life and mine, there is a day we are born and there is a day that we will leave the earth. No matter how fat your bank account is, or how many planes you may fly, there is a limitation placed upon humans, earth-born earth-suited man. It gives us a sense that we cannot make things out of ourselves without dependence on God. Then we said **a storm is an equalizer**. Storms equalize people. Whether rich or poor their fate is made the same when a storm rises. Storms do not stop at a poor man's house, neither do they stop at a rich man's house. When a storm comes it comes; the poor and the rich, just like rain, they benefit from them all. The Bible says that God rains upon the just and the unjust, so it means it is an equalizer. Recently we heard that in very noble places that you would think there would be no virus, like in the palace, who would think there would be a virus, finding its way to a palace and to a Prime Minister's life? Our current president as at the time of the writing of this book along with some of his family members also took a hit from the evil virus. Just as the poor people meet their fate in storms, so also do people of high strata in society. W**e see the demonstration of the power of God whenever there are storms**. We also say **storms remind us that God is the sole person in control of His universe**. We are not in control, God is. Sometimes we hold on to things that only

God can give us answers to, and we hold on in vain. For example, when flying an airplane you plunge into turbulence, and people freak out. All of us do, especially if it is very bad. Sometimes we think that the pilot does not know what they may be doing. They have trained for hours and flown for many hours. This is why particular companies entrust the lives of many people to them. The day I came to that resolve, I relaxed my nerves a bit. If you understand what turbulence does, it will also make you relax. I've often wondered why I will see people sleeping whereas there was a turbulence. I felt very annoyed at them that they were not panicking the way I was and some of them actually would be snoring through it unbeknownst to me, they had flown many, many times. They had seen worse turbulence, and there was one thing for sure and certain in them that they would get to their destination point. So whether the plane went up, it came down, it shook left and right, it descended 5000 feet and went up again, there were many bumps, they would sleep through it. They had seen it done before and had a customised T-shirt to show for it. When you have not been to a particular place before, you want to hold on as if you are in control. Let me remind you, you are not in control. God is in control. He's got the whole world in His hands. The expanse of this world, the galaxies of the universe, are under His watchful eye. God knows them by name, just as He knows the number of hairs upon your head, even including the ones you lost. He knows them. He knows the number. The Lord our God is not only all-knowing; He is all- powerful. You think you are powerful, but God is all-powerful. Sometimes as humans, when God puts a little drop of anointing on top of our backs, we think that we are the best thing that walked the earth. Yet there comes a time that God strips you to your bare nakedness and makes you know that you are helpless without Him, that He is the one who's got the whole world in His Hands. Not you, not me, not the systems, not governments, not society nor secret societies that think that they hold this world in ransom. By the way we are praying, not just as a church but as a collective Body of Christ, for societies that think that it is their agenda to dehumanize and downsize population on Earth, because they feel a particular ethnicity is not worth staying alive. This world belongs to Jehovah. All of us are in transit. It does not matter which country you live in. You may be born in a country, you may be born in some noble place, but someday, clearly, your remains shall be put into the ground. That tells us that we are limited and that there is someone bigger than you. There is a bigger God, a greater King, a greater Master, a supreme King. His power is greater than all. So God is essentially in control. Not you. Not myself. Not anyone. Glory be to God. God is in control.

Next, we shall teach about what to do in a storm. Storms will come. They will come for those of you who can speak 700 words per minute in tongues. They'll also come for those of you who do not pray in tongues. They will come for those of you who have been baptized and those who have not been baptized. They will come for those of you who have taken communion and those who have not taken communion. They will come for those of us who can see visions into the realms of God. They also come for those of you as blind as bats. But storms will come. I don't want to say when they come because the time apportioned for a storm to come may be different for someone as opposed to you. Sometimes somebody may be coasting very nicely from a home, and another person may be going through turbulence from the same home. Someone in the same church is enjoying a particular message and another person is frowning on it. Someone is being elevated by a message that brings the realness of life and makes life very practicable for them to live. Another person is thinking about what you may tell them about the pie in the sky. So, the when is not important. When they do come though, what are you going to do?

The first thing I want to impress upon you is **to learn to wait**. Learn to wait on God because the storms will come. I want to look at Psalm 27: 14:

Wait on the Lord,
Be of good courage, and He shall strengthen your
heart.
Wait, I say wait on the Lord.

Now there is no part of this verse where they put my name
there. There is no part where they put a ministry's name there.
Therefore you cannot blame a pastor, a deacon, a bishop or
a prophet. You cannot blame anybody for the duration of
your storm. You can only blame yourself in how you conduct
yourself in the process of your storm. The conduct of your
heart will determine how long you stay in the storm. The
Bible says to wait. Isaiah 40: 31 says "But those who wait".
It means that are people who will not wait. I pray you are
one of those who wait. There are people that say that if God
does not come through; they give God a certain time. If
God does not come through by a particular period in time,
they will fix it themselves. If you are going to fix it yourself,
then I'm going to tell you something. You are going to find
out in the end that you are making a big mess of your life.
Those who wait on the Lord, they are the ones that will renew
their strength. Not everyone can renew their strength in the
storm. It is only those who learn to wait. Those are the ones
that can renew their strength and they will mount up with
wings like eagles. They shall run and not be weary. They shall
walk and not faint. It is those who wait; it is not those who

are in a hurry. Waiting here does not mean doing nothing. Waiting here accepts the fact of dependence on God, that I cannot and will not take any initiative without consulting with God, or receiving counsel from godly counselors.

Habakkuk 2: 3 speaks to the vision. The reason to wait for the storm to pass for God to work your storm is that you cannot do anything about it, only God can.

> *The vision (or the desired thing) is for an*
> *appointed time,*
> *But at the end it shall speak and it will not lie.*
> *Though it tarries, wait for it.*

The vision will not lie or die, Amen, Praise God. Though it tarries, wait for it because it will surely come. It will not tarry. I have a message from the Lord for you. The message is that you cannot hurry God. You cannot hurry Him in fasting, you cannot hurry Him in seed sowing, you cannot hurry Him in anything. There is a time that God has set in the earth to do things (Ecclesiastes 3: 11), and when that time comes, it will be beautiful. Yes, He makes everything beautiful in its time. Also, He has put eternity in their hearts, except that no one can find out the work that God does from the beginning to the end. So God has made everything beautiful in its time. What should you do in a storm? Wait on the Lord. Waiting is the most difficult thing for any human being to do. When you have to wait at the airport for someone who has flown over to visit you, it becomes a very unnerving thing, especially for me. Where are they now? Did they get their bags? At which point are they now? Especially one hour, two hours, three hours later and they are not coming out. Are they lost? Did they get lost somewhere? Did they actually get on board? Were they on the flight? Another part of waiting that I don't quite like, is when I have flown from a very long distance and must wait again to be picked up. In both situations, I don't do too well, so you keep praying for me, okay? I mean, if somebody is going to arrive in two hours, I want to make sure I'm there an hour before and get a cup of coffee, sit down, and relax. I don't want them to get there and rather wait for me. Let's look at Galatians 4: 4, time is in God. Seed sowing preempts time, but it preempts you to the timing of God. Sacrifices preempt time, but they preempt you to the timing of the Lord. Father Abraham was told by Almighty God that he would have a son, and Abraham believed God, but in between his believing, he made a certain cardinal mistake. In the midst of all that God came to him, but God was waiting for something to eat from the hands of Abraham. Three men came to his tent. Even though God received something from Abraham, the Bible says that the men did not tell Sarah she would give birth tomorrow. They rather said a year from now. That puts an additional year on Sarah. Not nine months from now; a year from now. This means that Jehovah is the sole calendar holder and He executes times and seasons. The Bible says in Galatians 4: 5-6:

> *In the fullness of time, God sent forth His Son,*
>
> *born of a woman, born under the law, to redeem*
>
> *those who were under the law that we might receive the adoption as sons. And*
>
> *because you are sons God has sent forth the Spirit of His Son into your hearts, crying out, "Abba, Father!"*

Waiting is a difficult thing; waiting to be promoted, waiting to be married, waiting to have children, waiting to be recognized, waiting for the harvest of your business, waiting to be enlarged. It is a very difficult thing, but it is in this process that characters are formed, shaped and developed. The worst thing to do in a storm is to hurry because you may make a mistake and head the wrong direction. When you look at Psalm 37: 34 it says:

> *Wait on the Lord and keep His way,*
> *And He shall exalt you to inherit the land,*
> *When the wicked are cut off, you shall see it.*

I want to restate the importance of waiting in your storm and why it is critically important that you harness your soul and keep yourself in check. Friends and family members may be putting strain and stress on you but keep your emotions stable.

Job 14: 14 says:

> *If a man dies, shall he live again?*
> *All the days of my hard service I will wait till my*
> *change comes.*

Chapter Thirteen

YOUR HOUR OF CHANGE
HAS COME

N ow I want to prophesy to somebody out there, your change will come. Yes, your change will come. It will come quite unsuspectingly when you are not even looking for it. It will come when others have denounced the fact that you are in line for a miracle. It will come in the midst of a pandemic. It will come in the midst of trouble. It will come when your back hurts. It will come when your bank account is running on zero. Even though you may have received some stimulus you're still running on zero. It will come when the power of God sees that it is time, and when that time is up you will see the hand of God. Job says all the days of his hard service he would wait, because he knows that change comes from God. I prophesy now in the name of the Lord, by the Word of the Lord according to Job 14: 14, your change shall come and your hour shall not pass you by in the Name of Jesus Christ. There's a day comfort will be removed and when you can call on people and they would not answer you because they have not put proper value on you. There comes a day that you would wake up and find that there's been a translation. You are no longer looking for coins, but you are counting paper. When we say paper, we are not dealing with fifties; we are dealing in the hundreds and in the millions. Yes, God does these things. God can change a person's situation in the midst of their storm. You are going to have to learn to wait. We are not people that went through the crucible, from the Josephs to those who had to build computers in the garage. When you are going through your wilderness, not many people will give notoriety to your existence. My Bible records that when the Lord Jesus came out of the wilderness, the same people in the synagogue who denounced and defamed His teaching received Him as one who taught with power and authority. There is a time that God adds value. There is a time that God unleashes anointing upon our lives to go forward in His Name and do mighty things for the glory of God.

Psalm 62: 5 says:

> *My soul waits silently for God alone.*

Do you know why it says the soul waits silently for God alone? Because we are prone to activity. When there is no activity we think we are not doing much, however, silence is activity. In fact, for many of us, our problems started the moment we broke our silence. Our problems started when we opened our mouths. Silence is equally an activity. Do you know that silence is non-verbal communication? It is an art. Sometimes you may hear a lady say, but I didn't say anything. Yes, right. You did not say or express words. But your body language spoke volumes. A man may say, I didn't say anything. Yes, you may not have said anything, but your mannerisms, the way you walk, the way you conducted your body language expressively spoke something. Silence itself is an activity. There are people who cannot be silent in a room for more than five minutes. They think the world is coming to an end, so they have to turn on the television. They have to hear some sound. They have to go down the stairs. They have to come up. They have to go and eat pizza. They have to eat yoghurt. They have to close the refrigerator. They have to open it back. You know how many times I've opened the refrigerator and not gotten anything from it? Just looked and closed and went back, opened, looked and closed. Man is not well accustomed to silence. The waiting game is not a great game, and I'm not here to let you know that I have perfected it. We are all in that school. The worst thing to do is to try to develop something in the midst of a storm, when you cannot find your feet. When there is darkness in a room, the first thing to find is light, not to walk, because you may take a walk into a huge hole. Those who walk into a darkened room should have the presence of mind that when light is present, everything in that particular arena becomes available to them. But there are those who will not wait. They will just think they know the place beforehand so waiting becomes a problem.

Psalm 29 teaches us the importance of waiting on God. Lord please help us to wait. Make that your desperate cry to the heavens! This word 'wait' is a problem when it comes to communication skills. People think that good communication is when you speak. No, good communication is having the ability to listen to understand what is being communicated to you. Communication is 80% listening and 20% talking. Good communication is not: okay, finish your sentence so that I can also come in with mine. We are not in the courtroom; please lay down your weapons. Great communication is having a good listening ear. If you cannot understand what is being said to you, chances are that you may defend yourself about something that has not been said at all. Here, God makes us understand that He is a God over the storm. He is God over your storm, but He wants to culture your heart and my heart to the place of waiting. Psalm 29: 1-3 says:

> *Give unto the Lord, you mighty ones,*
> *Give the Lord glory and strength.*
> *Give unto the Lord, glory to His Name,*

Worship the Lord in the beauty of His Holiness.
The voice of the Lord is over the waters.
The God of glory, He thunders,
The Lord is over many waters.

It means that God's presence is known in the midst of your storm. The voice of the Lord is powerful. You cannot fret and fidget and hear the voice of God. You can only be still and know that He is God.

The voice of the Lord is powerful,
The voice of the Lord is full of majesty.
The voice of the Lord breaks the cedars.
Yes, He splinters the cedars of Lebanon.
He makes them also to skip like a calf,
Lebanon and Sirion like the wild young ox.
The voice of the Lord divides the flames of fire.
The voice of the Lord shakes the wilderness,
The Lord shakes the Wilderness of Kadesh.
The voice of the Lord makes the deer give birth,
And strips the forest bare;
In His temple, everyone says "Glory!".
(Psalm 29: 4-9)

The voice of God will help you to give birth. There are people pregnant with ideas. They are pregnant with dreams and visions and great aspirations, but there is a great storm, and because of the storm they cannot see their Canaan. However, I came as a prophet of hope to tell you that when you hear the sound of the voice of God and the timing of the Lord, you will give birth just like a deer gives birth. You will also give birth on time by the power of God.

Now Verse 10, is where I want to rest on very strongly: *The Lord sat enthroned at the Flood*, or at the storm. Let me put it in my language: the Lord rides upon your storm. The Lord sat enthroned upon your storm, upon your flood, upon all that garbage and nonsense going on around you, the Lord sits on top of it. The God of the universe is not dead. He is alive and well and his power is available to whosoever believes in Him. God is active and well in our universe. He is well informed about where we are in this COVID-19 situation. We may be surprised at the turn of events, but Jehovah is ahead of us. Jehovah is gone ahead of us. He sits enthroned upon the flood. God is bigger than your trouble. He is bigger than your storm. He is bigger than your disease. He is bigger than your financial problems. God is bigger than the situations you find yourself in. The Bible says, *And the Lord sits as King forever.* He sits as King forever. I know in my lifetime there are kings that have come and they have left. There are presidents that have come and they have left, but there is a King of kings and a Lord of lords, His name is Yahweh, Adonai, the El Shaddai, the Great God of the universe. God is actively alive in our lives if we are going to learn to wait on Him. The Bible says He sat enthroned on the flood. He's not absent; He's right on top of the flood. Oh yes. You are not going under.

Let us look at Psalm 69: 6:

> *Let not those who wait for You, O Lord of Hosts,*
> *be ashamed,*
> *Let not those who seek You be confounded.*

It means that waiting guarantees that you are not ashamed. If you wait and you seek God, you will not be ashamed, and you will not be confounded. So what do you do in a storm? Number One: you wait. You wait until your change comes (Job 14:14). It does not mean you do nothing. No, I'm not suggesting that. Sometimes it is good in a time of silence to get in prayer and to read the Word, but also to take a note-pad and begin to plan things on your thoughts, things that God may impress on you, long term goals and short term goals, like a ten year plan. Break them into five years, then break them into months. Things that you project to do. That does not mean they are going to happen exactly as written, but God can work with you because you have something. The Bible says that God orders the plans of a man (Psalm 37:23), but if you have no plan, He cannot order it. I asked a gentleman, what is your purpose in this marriage? He said

"Just to be married" with such seriousness. I asked another person, what is your purpose in this business you're going to do? He said, just to make money. So when you make the money, what next? He said, I've not thought about that. Well, you need to think about what you're going to do with the money, because if you don't think about it something will think it for you. So waiting is a good thing. When I was a lad, I thought people were trying to slow me down. I wanted to grow up fast. Then once I got my freedom, and was on my own, I thought this was the life I wanted to lead. I did not know that it came with a price. I didn't know that you have to find your own food. Back in the days we had to get carpenters to make our bed, and where I lived in my gracious apostolic room the regular bed size would not fit there. The carpenter literally had to come to a kitchen turned into a bedroom to size up the bed, and then I had to cut a foam mattress to make it like as a proper mattress. When you don't know where somebody has been, you may misjudge them. You may mischaracterize the whole situation and think that easy does it, easy gets it done. When you are a child, you think your parents are not sharp enough. When you grow older, you realize you were stupid enough. You are thinking of getting out of a situation. When you get out you realize it's not fun on the other end at all. There are those of us who wish we could go back to our childhood, but there's no going backwards. Even though some aged people act very infantile, there is no going backwards. Age is creeping up on you, so my friend, it is better you get with the program. God wants us to learn to wait. Now in Matthew Chapter 8, we read about when the Lord took his disciples to go to the other side of the Gadarenes. A storm did rise, and Jesus was in the boat. There are many that make us think that Christianity is devoid of storms, that is not true. The Lord Jesus was not handed a certificate. He was handed nails in His hands, pierced on His side and His feet. The Bible says of the Lord Himself saying, if you can suffer with Me, then and only then can you reign with me as also alluded by Apostle Paul in (2Timothy 2:12). When did we depart from true biblical teachings and giving many false hopes.

Chapter **Fourteen**

THE THING CALLED LIFE

This is real life. This thing called life, we are doing it. We are living it. I'm not saying don't be hopeful. I'm a preacher of faith. I'm saying that your anchor must hold strong because storms do come, but what do you do when the storms come? The Bible says a storm blew, and the winds beat against their boat. Now what has waiting got to do with this? No matter how long the storm blew, at the end of the day the storm stopped. For as long as they knew that the Lord was with them, no matter how long it took, the storm came to an end. Your storms will also come to an end in the Name of the Lord. Every storm has a natural duration, but when Yahweh steps into it, He cuts it into two because He rides Himself upon the storms. He establishes and enthrones Himself upon the storm. There is a true story I'm about to share with you. There was a young man that a particular somebody didn't really like. This young man took ill, and everybody thought he was going to die. They took him to the hospital. The place they took this young man to was the same place this lady worked as a nurse. This lady would mix DDT (if you know what DDT is, it is worse than Dettol; it is poison) in his food. The young man as hungry as he was and weak and frail would eat it all. After a month or so, she saw the man was not dying. In fact, he was getting better, so she increased the DDT. One day when she went to work, the man was not in his bed anymore. They both belonged to the same church. The next Sunday this young man was giving a testimony of how that by God's power somebody fed him with sumptuous meals and through the food he got healed. The DDT killed everything! Please don't practice this. I am not suggesting by any means that DDT and Dettol and Lysol will do that. I am only saying if people wish you harm and evil God will turn it around. When we were coming of age, we had many storms. One of the storms I faced was a curse that said I would never be able to buy a bag of rice and not enjoy the comfort of a ceiling fan. I'm here to tell you that I can buy as many bags of rice I want, and I'm not fidgeting with a fan. I can sleep in an air conditioned room. God will ride your storm. God will give you power over your storm. In the storm, we see fearful disciples, just like we also can be fearful when we are told we have a very bad disease or something that's about to take us out. But when we invite Jesus, when we invite the Master, when we invite the One who cuts everything in two, when we invite the Man of Galilee, when we invite the King of kings into that situation, what the doctors cannot do, He can. What the judge cannot rule in your favor, He can. What the bank cannot do in your favor, He can. What the loan officer has disqualified you for, there is another company that will help you, for the power of God is not limited. God is not limited. Glory to God, He is not limited. We serve an unlimited God. So the tide will abate. Wait, your boat will get on shore and anchor. No matter how long it takes, you are going to see the glory and the power of God. No matter how many years it takes, you are going to see the fulfillment of the Word of the Lord. No matter how long it takes, you are going to see the Word of the Lord. It was a prophet that said though the vision tarry, wait for it, it will come to pass. Whoever thought a sickly boy at the age of seven would live to these glory years? Whoever thought that the globe would be asking for me? What God does is He hides you in the storm. What man does is he wants you to be found in that storm. When I lived down south for almost six years I cried to the Spirit of God, Lord, why are you hiding me here in this little place? One day I heard it very clear, to develop you. Boy, that was some development. There is a time of God earmarked for each and every one. Sometimes somebody may keep someone's ministry under a bushel, so they never rise. But when your time comes, no one can do anything about it. Back in the day, as young as I was, there were grown-ups who would sit and wait and go and have a conference about me, so that it would create enmity between me and my spiritual father. There are people whose sole aim and ambition is to create such things so you will never arrive at where you must. But let me tell you, like Joseph, you may be left in the pit for dead, but there is a band of Ishmaelites who are going to carry you on their caravan. They are going to take you to your place of the promise. Yes, they may throw you into jail forgotten, but your gift is going to lift you and place you with people in places of honor. That is the power of God at work. God is not a man to recuse Himself from an individual that waits upon Him. The Bible says those that wait upon the Lord shall renew their strength. They shall mount up with wings like the eagle.

Chapter Fifteen

WHAT SHOULD I DO
IN A STORM?

What should you do in a storm? Firstly, I said you should, wait on God. Learn to draw out plans; long- and short-term goals. Learn to be creative around the times that nothing seems to be happening. Put out applications. It is all a part of the process of your waiting. The time will come when somebody who knows somebody will speak for you. Secondly, reacting to any storm through emotional decisions can actually keep you there longer. You need **emotional stability**. No one can be spiritually balanced and not emotionally stable. Give me anybody who can rise into spiritual heights without emotional stability. I can almost certainly without batting an eye tell you that there is danger ahead for them. Emotional stability is a priority. That is why you must not allow anyone to govern your emotions negatively to where you become someone that you are not. If you are a lover, keep loving. Let the haters hate, but you keep loving. If you are a giver, don't become a miser; keep giving. Never allow yourself to be emotionally bankrupt, because when a storm arises and your emotions are haywire, you are going to take decisions from people whom you should be teaching. You do not react to a storm. A storm is like an argument. The more you react to it, the more you give it power to fan itself in your face. You rest in the storm. God will pull you out. We end with Matthew 8: 24-26. The emotions of these disciples were all haywire. Fear, anxiety, confusion, perplexity, hopelessness, abandonment, everything all in a pot was mixed up. In fact, one of them had the audacity to say to the Lord, don't you care that we perish? Now what about the Lord? People can be so selfish! Jesus was in the boat with them. If the boat overturned He would have drowned too. Thank God for overlooking our selfish tendencies. The disciples did not seem concerned about the fact they were in the same boat with Jesus. We are perishing they said. We don't know about you. We don't know what's going to happen to you. We don't actually care what may happen to you, but for now we are perishing. You have got to do something. It is very much like people of our days. They don't know the pastor praying for them also has a need. They do not know that pastors are human beings also. But Jesus says to them, why are you fearful? Now fear is an emotion. Oh, you of little faith. That means that when you give a platform to a negative emotion, it will impact your faith. It will allow you to have no faith or little faith. When you give attention to reason, you will never operate in faith, because faith believes that the invisible God can create substance out of nothing. Faith does not rely on us. It relies on the potency of God's Word, that we can lean on the power of the Word of God, that God is, and that God is faithful. Because He is faithful, he will not deny Himself of that attribute as to what He is. He said to them, why are you fearful? O you of little faith. Now, fear and faith cannot cohabit. The more fearful you are, the less faith you have. The more you give in to the storm, the more fearful you shall become. I have known of individuals whom a doctor told very clearly that they were going to die. They gave them three months, six months, and they lived on 15 years. There is no rubber stamp under your foot and there are no dates imprinted anywhere. Only Jehovah has the last say-so, so do not be afraid. When the storms arise, allow God to hold your emotions in place. Don't be helter-skelter, making decisions borne out of fear, but rather out of faith that God can, and God will. Don't react to your storm. Rest in the invisible power of God and the promises of God. God is able, God is able. So we leave you with two words. The first word is to **WAIT**. The second word is to **REST**. Come to the place of absolute rest in your emotions that our God reigns. He arose in the same thing they were afraid of and mastered authority over the situation. The Bible says, He rebuked the winds and the sea and there was great calm. I want to ask a question: couldn't the disciples have done that? You say No, they couldn't. Then why is it that they went out two by two, and they were driving out demons and showing the power of God? Why they were able to demonstrate kingdom power over demons and could not have authority over this is because they allowed their emotions to have a front seat. Do not use yesterday's glory as a badge of honor for today. The people of Israel in the great wilderness were told by Jehovah to collect manna daily (manna means 'what is this?") but they thought they could turn things around, just in case there was no supply. And so they collected more, and what was 'what is it' became 'what are these worms'. When you step outside the realms of the confines of what God has spoken peace into, you shall also find worms. You shall find detestable things. You shall find things outside the perimeter of the provision of God. He will take care of you today. You say what about tomorrow? It hasn't come yet. He will take care of you tomorrow too. What about ten years to come? He will take care of you. Now, have you been to tomorrow before? No. Have you been to ten years ahead before? No. But God is in the future and He knows it is going to be all right. I prophesy by the sound of the Living God, that this pandemic will not take you like a storm over, but you are going to rise above it. In fact, the better of you is coming out of the storm, and you are going to rise above it, by the power of God. I prophesy the life, power and the anointing of God will rest upon you. The goodness of Jehovah shall be with you and shall be yours.

Chapter Sixteen

FAVOR IN THE
MIDST STORMS

We are going to investigate the Book of Acts, Chapter number 27 is going to become our key text.

We are dealing with favour, in the midst of storms. How is it possible to have divine favor in the midst of storms? The pandemic is not the only storm people are facing. There are people that do not and have not caught the virus, but they have other storms in their lives. All the stocks and bonds and everything that they placed their future on all of a sudden seem to have dissipated into thin air, so as someone is dealing with the virus, another person is worried about money, or the security of their future. Another person may be dealing with a wayward child. No matter what you did, prayed, fasted, and you sought God. You sought counsel. You have done all the things you know to do, but there seems to be no way to the end. God will favor you in the midst of your storms. Favor is not coming; Favor is here. Favor is not something we feel; favor is something we experience. You may feel a lot of things working against your favor. You may feel a lot of situations working against what you set out to do. You may feel as if you are standing in the same station in life, but our Heavenly Father, the God of all Favor, the God of all grace, will grace you. When God graces you He greases you. When God puts His divine ability on you, He also puts oil on you for performance. You are able to do what you could not do before. Paul says even in his trials, where there was a thorn caught in his flesh, God said to him, my grace is sufficient for you. Grace is always sufficient. Favor satisfies anything that cannot and will not be satisfied in life. The grace of God does. The favor of God does. The word 'grace' comes from the Greek derivation *Charis* which also is interpreted 'Favor'. Therefore, when we say grace and favor, we are saying the same things, just using different wording. May God of all Favor bless you in Jesus' Name.

Psalm 5: 12.

> *For You, O Lord, will bless the righteous*
> *With favor You will surround him as with a shield.*

So favor is a buffer zone. There are many who are informed about the strategies of warfare and there are buffer zones or zones that have no entry points. We could use North Korea and South Korea as an example. There is a line of demarcation between them that you cannot cross. Favor does that; it lifts up a shield. When the enemy would have attacked, the favor of the grace of God disallows the enemy to carry on the fullest intent of the onslaught. The Lord will bless the righteous and with favor encompass him like a shield. Psalm 30: 5 reads:

> *For His anger endureth but for a moment;*
> *His favor is for life.*

Now for those of you who think eschatologically that we are at a place where the world should end today and tomorrow, I need you to understand that God holds the world in His Palm. Neither you nor I know the time. We can speculate, we can think through the lenses of Scripture, but remember that we see through a glass dimly. When He who should come should come then we will gain understanding about times. That means though that we are drawing closer to that day, but as to pointedly pinpoint the day, we do not know the hour. We live as though He may come tomorrow or tonight. Now watch what the scripture says. It says His anger is but for a moment. So if you are suggesting that this pandemic is the exhibition of the anger of God, I want to tell you according to His own word, that His anger is for a moment. The Bible says that His favor is for life. That means that in our storm favor seems far bigger and stronger than the storm itself. It says weeping may endure for the night, but joy comes in the morning. The day light is far longer than the night time so the pandemic, the virus, the disease, that trouble in your home, that trouble in your health, that situation that you may be going through; I need you to know that that thing, its duration, its set time is far shorter than the blessing that God is going to birth out of it. But one must set their heart right. There is a whole lot that goes on in the human chamber in the time of comfort. When there is comfort, we do not blame God that we have comfort, but when there is trouble unjust humans point their little fingers to the face of Jehovah, that He is the cause of it. When we were enjoying good economy, good health, peace on every end no one blamed God, no one credited it to Him. It seemed as though it was a normal part of human life. Then when something evil hits, atheists, agnostics, people that ridicule church folks and people who don't believe in God and believe that there is a real God and His Son is Jesus, begin to say that God is behind the evil. Why do you not also say that He is behind the good? Don't we see that good is far more pronounced and greater than evil? When we turn on our news channels we are stuck and glued to them because they sell fear. Fear is a great seller. When someone tells you that you are going to die, nobody wants to die. People want some level of release. The person telling you about dying will also die one day, you are more likely to do something about it. No one will be here permanently. So understand that the moment of your storm is far shorter than the length of your favor. God will favor Zion. He will favor His people. Just structure your heart properly. Get your heart in the right mood and in the right position. Psalm 30: 7 says,

> *Lord, by favor, Thou hast made my mountain to*
> *stand strong.*
> *Thou didst hide Thy face, and I was troubled.*

In the Bible when mountains are mentioned, it is either a reference to a literal mountain (like Mount Nebo, Mount Ararat, Mount Gerizim or Gethsemane etc.) or mountains represent problems or kingdoms. Here, it represents authority and kingdom. The scripture says the Lord has made my kingdom strong. May God forever make your kingdom strong during critical and dire situations in the Name of the Lord Jesus Christ, by His eternal power. Then we come to Psalm 44: 3:

> *For they got not the land in possession by their*
> *own sword,*
> *Neither did their own arm save them,*

But Thy right hand and Thine arm, and the light
of Thy countenance
Because You favored them.

You have not gotten to where you are to in life because of your education. There are people who are more educated than you and me. There are people who are far advanced than you are. You are where you are by reason of the grace of God. May the right hand of the Lord be extended toward you and me in Jesus' Name. The arm of the Lord is outstretched towards you today. The psalm also talks about the light of God's countenance. You see, when the light of God's countenance spreads upon a person, darkness dissipates. It leaves them. Darkness, bleak, dire straits, pandemics, viruses, diseases, infirmities, troublous times, storms that rise, begin to break and disintegrate and leave them because God has favored them. May God favor you in the Name of the Lord Jesus Christ! May the favor of Heaven be upon you! When you go out, may you be favored! Is this preacher talking about favor in the time of a storm? Yes, I'm talking about favor not after the storm, but in the midst of the storm.

May someone remember you! A few days ago, I got a call from one of my daughters, and it was a very interesting call. She asked where I was and I told her I was praying in the church. She then asked if it was okay to stop by at a particular time. I wanted to know the exact reason. Friends, there are no small blessings. If somebody can go out there and shop and get you food to eat, it is a blessing. Upon reaching home, I found that they had already gone ahead and sent the blessing! The Lord God who fed the Prophet by the Brook Cherith, the Lord God who fed him by ravens, will feed you too. Now let me tell you something about ravens that you may not have thought about. First, they are very unclean animals. Secondly, they do not share, so a raven will not bring you a burger. A raven will not serve you meat and go hungry. But when God commands your raven to bring you your safe haven, to bring you your meal, to bring you what you should eat, what you shall rest upon, when God breaks his countenance upon you, God will favor you by His mighty power. The arm of the Lord is lifted for somebody today, wherever you are, and wherever you stand, in the Name of the Lord. Wherever you stand, by the power of God, the light of God shall break upon you. You shall see the light of life. It is possible to walk in this world and not see the light of life. Folks, we are not in control of anything. Only Jehovah is. There are people who chaperone over little positions and little things they have. You must vacate that arena and let God take preeminence over that area. It does not matter if they make you a boss over this or that. Jesus Christ, the Son of the living God, is Boss over all! Right now you may have money, but you cannot fly. You may have money, but you cannot go on vacation. You may have money, but you cannot do the things you want to do. That tells you that humankind is limited by certain things and by certain constraints. In the midst of this limitation is where God the Almighty comes to show Himself as a sovereign God, as a commander of the universe, as the one who extends the courtesy of His favor to a person who is in the dunghill, to make them a prince to stand upon a place where princes only ride. May Jehovah favor you in the Name of the Lord Jesus in this season! May anything that has cocooned, encapsulated and entombed you give way to angelic presence with brilliance of the light of God. Hear me and hear me loud and clear. In the midst of the mess there will be a message. God, our Heavenly Father, will triumph in you in the midst of trials, and He will put a placard on top, that He is Jehovah Nissi The Lord shall be there. You did not get that job by your own way. Yes, your resume is right, but there were better resume ahead of you. It was not because you were that beautiful, all set and well put together. It was because God favored you.

> *Psalm 102: 13-14 is one of my favorite scriptures. It says:*
> *He will arise and have mercy on Zion,*
> *For the time to favor her, yes, the set time,*
> *has come.*

Now, the question is to be asked, when was this spoken of? This was spoken of when they were in captivity. But it says He will arise and have mercy on the people that dwell in Zion, for the time to favor her had come. Yes, there is a set time for storm and there is a set time for favor. We have entered into our season of favor. In the Name of the Lord Jesus, this virus shall die in the face of the earth, and God Almighty shall give our scientists and our researchers knowledge for a cure in the Name of the Lord. God will sovereignly, supernaturally and completely erase this Corona Virus by His mighty power.

Chapter Seventeen

UNDERSTAND YOUR
NEED FOR PRAYER

In Psalm 102: 14, the scripture continues:
For Your servants take pleasure in her stones, and
show favor to her dust.

Psalm 106: 4 says:
Remember me O Lord, with the favor Thou
bearest unto Thy people
O visit with me with Thy salvation.

Someone needs to cry out to God: O Lord, remember me! It is not as if He has forgotten your name, but you need to cry the ancient cry "Remember me!" Jabez prayed God to remember him. Jephthah prayed for God to remember him. People who were forgotten in the pages of the Bible, prayed to God to remember them. May the Father remember you in Jesus' Name. Proverbs 3: 3-4 says:

Let not mercy and truth forsake you.
Bind them around your neck, write them on the
tablet of your heart,
And so find favor and high esteem in the sight of
God and man.

If you are not undergirded with mercy and truth (Verse 3) you will not find favor. When the scripture asks you not to let them forsake you it means walk with this because Verse 4 says you will find favor. So favor can be found by practicing mercy and truth. See how Joseph was sold and now lands in Egypt. Through a series of events, he is thrown into prison and out of prison, he is esteemed and lifted high. When his brothers came to him, the reason why he was promoted and preserved was because he had the girdle of mercy and truth on his side. Many of us want to exact punishment when God causes us to rise and come into a prominent position. You want people to know that you are all that and a bag of chips. Understand that if you do not walk in mercy, you are not on God's strength. You have to walk in mercy and also in truth. The Bible says you will find favor and you will find high esteem in the sight of God and also with men. The Bible says in Proverbs 13: 15,

Good understanding gains favor.

It means if you lack understanding, you can dismiss favor.
If you lack understanding, you will misbehave. There are
people who see a person that is supposed to be given honor
and respect, but they sit back as though they themselves need
to be respected. When you walk with that attitude you have
misjudged understanding. When a noble person walks into
a room, everybody stands because it is in honor of the office
the person stands. It is only a fool who will keep on doing
the same things they are doing and getting the same results,
but a wise person gains understanding. When you gain understanding you gain favor. So quit praying for favor when
the culture of your heart is not seeking understanding in the
rules of engagement for life and how to conduct oneself. You
see a young pastor talking to an older man. Because God
gave them oil, they talk to an older man as if he is their child,
and feel proud that they are calling them 'Papa'. It is because
they lack understanding. Someday, the favor that God has
given you will be taken. If you misjudge times and seasons
and proper protocols, you will lose favor. There are protocols
to be observed. When you walk into any edifice, there is a
protocol in place. You do not do what you wish or want.
According to Romans 13, God is the one who institutes order
in society. He who resists that ordinance resists God and
brings damnation to themselves. I have heard many times
from various people: "No, without me that business cannot
stand, without me that church cannot go on, without me

those children can never become anything, without me…."
Without you? You have poor understanding. Without God!
So get good understanding. Through the years, you will
come to find that the person you put down and downgraded
becomes somebody. Yes, parents do that sometimes. They
pick on one of their children and think that they would never
arrive at any place, but that child becomes their hope in the
end. May you solve somebody's problems by the power of
God in Jesus' Name.

Now we go to Acts 27. It is a long passage and I'm going to
pick certain things from it. Here is the apostle Paul setting
sail to Italy as one of a group of prisoners being delivered
by the Augustan Regiment. Verse 3 notes that Julius treated
Paul kindly. Julius treated Paul with mercy, a sign of good
understanding. He gave Paul liberty to go to his friends to
receive care so that his friends could minister to his needs. In
Verses 7 and 8 we are introduced to the coming of the wind
which causes the group to sail in great difficulty. It says the
wind would not permit them. In some versions it says it is
an ordinary breeze. It is not talking about a great tornado
on the onset, but it starts with the wind not permitting
them. It gets to a point where sailing becomes dangerous,
and Paul advises them (Verses 9 and 10). Look, you may
be a prisoner among people, but you are the one that God
graced. This was an accurate perception by the great Apostle

Paul. Nevertheless, the centurion was more persuaded by the helmsman and the owner of the ship than by Paul. There are people that are far more interested in natural things and in physical observances than things that are much more of spiritual matter. Whilst we are waiting for a vaccine, can the church engage in prayer which is spiritual and see the Hand of God also in operation? Verse 13 then says the south wind blew softly. Sometimes the enemy comes in softly. When you begin to sense a soft breeze of the enemy, that is a time to engage the presence of God. Supposing that they had obtained their desire, they thought Okay, this is just going to be nothing but just a soft wind. This is natural. That's no big deal. Don't listen to that Paul. Don't listen to him that there's trouble coming. After all, if God prophesied anything, it has to be always good. Who told you that? It goes on to say that not long after that a tempestuous headwind arose. If you know what a headwind is, when you are in a plane and all of a sudden, you begin to dance around in the plane? That's a headwind. It was so intense that the ship was caught and could not head into the wind so they let her drive. Basically, there was nothing they could do in the storm. They had no control over it. The captains could not do anything. They could not steer in the storm. You cannot steer in a storm. It is only God who rides a storm! Because a strong wind arose, they were shaken and could not control the ship. The captain, the ones that held the prisoners, the centurion, everybody was in the same boat. Isn't it strange? That the prisoner and person walking outside free are both under the mercy of the pandemic? We are all in the same boat. But there is mercy coming from the throne of God. There is power coming from the throne of God. Now verse number 22 says, *I urge you to take heart*. This is Paul who told them that there would be all kinds of things in the storm. The boat and the cargo would be lost and probably human life would also be lost.

Now he urges them to take heart for there would be no loss of life among them, only of the ship. Now you may say that, well, maybe Paul is giving a wrong prophecy here. No, God speaks per time. At a particular time the Lord may say something, and then a few days later the Lord can change it. A clear example is about a king that God sent the prophet Isaiah, to go tell him to prepare and put things in order, for he was going to die. The Bible says this king turned his face towards the Lord and he cried out to God that God would remember how he had walked in integrity, and how he had served the Lord. Whilst the great, notable, aristocratic prophet was just about leaving the court of the king, the voice of Elohim came on to the Prophet again, to go back and tell the king that He was going to add 15 more years to his life. Now wasn't God the one who told the prophet Isaiah to tell Hezekiah he was going to die? Wasn't

Isaiah a notable prophet? Wasn't his ministry known to be quite an outstanding one? Isaiah in his day spoke about the coming of the Messiah. Isaiah in his day spoke about the virgin that would incubate the God Man. Isaiah in his day spoke prophetically about the timeline, not only about the coming of Jesus, but about the last things and the last events of life. But just like Isaiah, Paul encourages them to take heart for no one would die, only the ship. Why only the ship? That was what they trusted in much. God is about to remove unnecessary defenses, because He is your defense, and He is your preserver, and He will share His glory with nobody. God will let you know that without Him we can do nothing. Paul affirms that God's presence stood by him (verse 23). He does not belong to the angel who stood by him. He belongs to and serves the God who sent the angel. God promises he will definitely stand before Caesar, so he urges the men to take heart, *for I believe God that it will be just as it was told me*. I also believe God, that there will be favor in the midst of the storm. I also believe God, that there will be healings in the midst of the storm. I also believe God for provision, I believe Him for promotion, I believe Him for elevation. I believe Him for security. I believe Him for resurrection power. I believe Him for His anointing. I believe Him for increment of wisdom and anointing in the Name of the Lord, I believe God! Therefore, take heart. Take heart, take heart. Initially he had said that the boat, the cargo and human life would be lost. Now, you are going to find out why there was a change. Remember, he had earlier predicted there would be loss, but 14 days later (Verse 27) he is telling them there would be no loss. You are going to find out that they were all under compulsory fasting. All of them, yes, because he would tell them to eat (in Verse 33). When you are in a storm, you do not have an appetite. When you are in a storm, there is no desire for pleasure. It is natural because God wants you in the storm to draw to Him. Many people misunderstand that. They do not have good understanding. They think God wants them to draw to their sorrow. God wants you at that time in the storm to rather draw closer to Him. You remember Nineveh, the land that was supposed to be under judgment? When Jonah preached there, he expected nothing but the judgement of God. But the Bible says that Nineveh proclaimed a fast and a place that is supposed to have come under judgement had judgement averted, and God began to favor Nineveh. May God do the same for you in a season as we wait upon the presence of God! Paul continues to encourage his terrified shipmates and he takes bread, gives thanks to God in the presence of them all, and begins to eat. Then they were all encouraged and took food too. Now, watch this. There was food on the ship, but they had no appetite to eat. What good is money when your body is riveted with cancers? What good is position when you're on a dying bed? May God give us good understanding. Now we get a headcount in Verse 37: 276 persons on the ship, and not one person was lost. Not one person reading this book and your family will be lost by the power of the living God. You say, those are bold statements. Yes, I would rather be bold than be beggarly. The power of God makes us roar like lions. We can defeat the enemy only by good understanding, by mercy and the girdle of truth. See, one time also in Mark 5, the disciples of Jesus arrived in a region where there was a possessed man, a man in the region of the Gadarenes.

Chapter Eighteen

CALL ON THE LORD JESUS

In Mark 4 as they had sailed, a wind rose up against them, and beat against the boat. When they realized they had no control (these were fisher folk who understood the rudiments of fishing, and about the sea, storms and all that), they called on Him who had control over the situation. His Name is Jesus. His Name is above every name. His Name is above cancer. His Name is above diabetes. His Name is above hypertension. His Name is above any chronic disease. His Name is above this coronavirus. His Name is above every storm in your life. His Name above any addiction you may be in. His Name is above every other name. His Name is above asthma. His Name is above acne. His Name is above any other known disease or predicament on the face of the earth. The Name Jesus is above all! All hail the Name of Jesus! All hail His Glorious Name! Sometimes we think our churches are great. No, our churches are not great. It is Jesus who makes His own great. It is Jesus who makes a man or a woman great. It is Jesus who makes a boy or girl great. He is our Anchor in the midst of the storm. He is our Shield in the midst of fiery darts. He is the Lord, our storm keeper. He is the Lord God who keeps us in the midst of danger. He is the Holy One of Israel. He is the Lord God who keeps us in a safe harbor. He is our God, our King, our Master. He is the Savior of the world. He is the Soon-returning King. He is the Great I Am. He is the Bread of Life. He is the Living Bread. He is the Lawgiver, Jesus the Holy One of Israel. He is the Healer. He is the Baptizer of the Holy Ghost. He is Jesus, the Son of the Living God. Bartimaeus knew him as the Son of David, but we know him as the Son of the Living God. He is the Messiah. He is the Lion of the tribe of Judah. He is the King of kings and the Lord of lords. He is the Alpha, the Omega, the Beginning and the End. He is my Rose of Sharon, the Lily of the Valley. He is the Bright and Morning Sun. His Name is Jesus. Oh how the angels in the early pages of Matthew, how they could not wait, how they could not wait to announce that Name! It that had been on their lips in the Heavenlies, how they could not wait! For unto us a Son shall be born, He shall be called Emmanuel. That which is conceived of thee, sayeth the Scripture, shall be by the Holy Ghost, and He shall be called Jesus, for He will save his people from their sins.

Friends, you can experience favor amid your storm. When Jesus is invited into that storm, He will quiet that storm, and He will lift your head up for His Name. Right now, in the Name of the Lord Jesus, any power that mimics the voice of God to control your emotions negatively, may they now vacate the arena to where they have gathered themselves. Any power that is illicitly and illegally operating in your life, may their powers be broken down to pieces in the Name of the Lord! The Hand of the Lord is lifted, and His mighty power is lifted. The Lord on high He is mighty, mighty to deliver. Some people have said, by the time this whole coronavirus is over many churches would be closed. I speak under unction, by the power of God, No! The church shall become as the scripture said: there shall be a hill within the hill. And the last day the mountain of the Lord shall be lifted up above other mountains, and others, other people shall run into the mountain and shall find security. I prophesy in the Name of the Lord, the church house is going to be full because people are looking not for a dead Jesus on a cross, but a Living Christ that can cross their crisis, a Living Redeemer that can save their souls. The power of God is running over pastors and preachers, because they are in the hiding seeking God. They are praying now. They are fasting now. They are in the hiding, they are studying now. Yes, the storms may arise, but there is a Name that anchors us in the midst of our storm. And the church house, in China, they are bolting churches up like the Zion Church. They have closed its doors because it is the agenda to shut the mouths of people. When they closed the doors the people came outside and did church. When they attacked them outside, they had now gathered in their homes. You cannot shut the Church of God down. No, you cannot shut the Army of the Living Christ down. Nero tried that and he failed. You cannot shut anything down. It is power from above. When the great curtain is about to be drawn, there will be a sound from Heaven by mighty angels. Yes, there will be a sound from Heaven. We know it is not time because we are still here. The Church is the only reason why danger and trouble and tumult have not reared its highest ugliest head. The Church is the reason why the Holy Spirit is still in the earth. The Church, the Ecclesia, is the reason why you are preserved. We are the Ark. Jesus is a container. He is the One that contains the Ark and He is bringing all of us into the safety vault of the Ark. We are going to sail over the storm like Noah, for a day is appointed for a cessation of trouble. As sure as trouble came and as sure as the storm came, there is a day that Almighty God will say enough is enough. Right now, in the midst of this mess, we shall yet see the power of God and the glory of the King, Hallelujah!

NOTES

NOTES